CROCHET
SECRETS
—— from ——
THE *Knotty* BOSS

CROCHET SECRETS

from

THE *Knotty* BOSS

**OVER 100 TIPS & TRICKS TO
IMPROVE YOUR CROCHET**

ANNA LEYZINA

DAVID & CHARLES
— PUBLISHING —

www.davidandcharles.com

CONTENTS

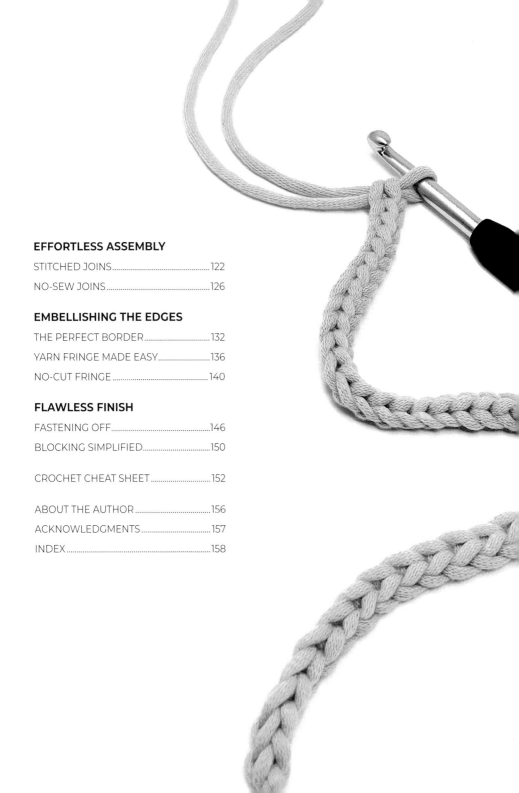

!

BEFORE WE BEGIN

This book is written using US crochet terms. Use the Cheat Sheet at the back of the book to convert these to UK terms if needed.

INTRODUCTION

"I am all for standards and traditions, but if we know that seamless joins exist, why is that not the standard way?"

If you understood that sentence, on a literal or emotional level, congratulations, this book is for you!

Over the years I learned many different tips and techniques that helped me deal with pesky crochet issues and annoyances. Things that were never taught as part of standard crochet, even though they should be. Whether it's foundation or finishing, working in rows or in the round, this is my comprehensive collection of tips and hacks that have helped me become a better crocheter and made me say, "Why were we not taught this sooner?"

Whether you're a beginner wanting to master some basic crochet techniques, or a seasoned garment crocheter looking to try your hand at amigurumi, you'll find tips to help make your life easier.

The book is broken down into sections, which cover various stages of crochet: from starting knots to finishing, and everything in between. Keep it handy to use as a quick reference guide when starting new projects or finishing up an old work-in-progress.

XO

THE
ESSENTIALS

—

A QUICK GUIDE TO SELECTING THE PERFECT
YARN AND TOOLS FOR THE JOB

CROCHET HOOKS

Not all hooks are created equal. Selecting the right hook is as important as selecting the right yarn. Sure, you can probably crochet with any hook, but there's nothing worse than using a hook that constantly slips, splits or pulls. Having the correct hook for the job can make your crocheting experience so much more enjoyable.

ANATOMY OF A HOOK

Crochet hooks might seem nothing more than a hook at the end of a straight stick, but there's more to a hook than that. In addition to having distinct parts, that perform specific functions, the hooks also come in two distinct styles.

Tapered hooks have a more rounded head that extends past the shaft. With a bowl that is more shallow than that of an inline hook.

Inline hooks have a more pointed head that is in line with the shaft. The bowl of an inline hook is much deeper than that of its tapered counterpart.

There are pros and cons to using either of the styles, what it boils down to is your own preference. Try them both out and see which works best for you.

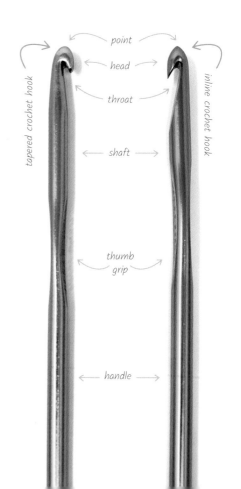

HOLDING THE HOOK

There's no "right" way to hold a crochet hook. The most common ways are referred to as the PEN and KNIFE hold, as they resemble how you typically would hold a pen or a knife. However, the best advice I can give is to hold it whichever way is most comfortable for you.

LEFT-HANDED
CROCHETERS
—
Hold up a mirror to the side of the photo. The reflected mirror image will show a left-handed view.

pen hold

knife hold

CHOOSING YOUR HOOK

Crochet hooks come in a variety of sizes, styles and materials. Here are some basics to consider when deciding on which hook to select for your next project.

Straight metal hooks

Metal hooks are durable, come in an array of basic sizes, and can be used for anything from garments to amigurumi. They make a great starter hook because they are widely available and generally more affordable.

Wooden hooks

Made from various woods, these hooks are typically lighter in weight than metal hooks. Great to use with slippery, non-organic fibers, because they provide more friction. Due to the fragile nature of the material they do not come in small sizes.

Straight plastic/resin hooks

A great basic alternative, especially if you need a jumbo size hook. They are very lightweight and offer a yarn grip similar to that of a wooden hook. Since they are more fragile they are typically not offered in the very small sizes.

Ergonomic hooks

Made in all types of materials, these hooks include a large handle that can provide a more comfortable grip, depending on how you hold your hook (see Holding the Hook).

Micro hooks

Steel hooks under 2mm (US size 4) in size that are typically used with very fine yarn or crochet thread.

Other hooks

This includes jumbo hooks, Tunisian crochet hooks, double-ended and travel hooks.

HOOK SIZES

MM	US
2.25	B-1
2.75	C-2
3.25	D-3
3.5	E-4
3.75	F-5
4	G-6
4.25	G
4.5	7
5	H-8
5.5	I-9
6	J-10
6.5	K-10.5
8	L-11
9	M/N-13
10	N/P-15
15	P/Q
16	Q
19	S
25	T/U/X

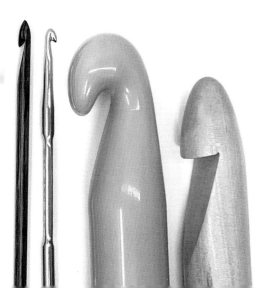

YARN

From natural fiber to acrylic, from super fine to extra bulky, from textured to smooth, the range of yarn options is limitless. Picking the appropriate yarn for your project can greatly affect the shape and construction of your finished piece. But don't forget to consider use and care.

LABELS ARE
YOUR FRIENDS

Learn to read a standard yarn label. From tool sizes to care instructions, weight, length and dye lot number, yarn labels hold all the important information.

LOST LABEL? NO PROBLEM!

If you have yarn without a label and need to quickly figure out its weight, you may easily do so by calculating the wraps per inch (WPI) or 2.5cm.

Instructions

1. Wrap the yarn around a ruler, or any other object such as a pen or crochet hook (A, B).

2. Count how many wraps it takes to cover one full inch (2.5cm).

3. See the Yarn Weight Calculations chart to calculate the weight of the yarn.

YARN WEIGHT CALCULATIONS

Yarn weight	Wraps per inch (2.5cm)
#1 Lace (1 ply)	30–40
#2 Sock, Fingering (2 or 3 ply)	15–30
#3 Sport weight (4 ply)	14–18
#4 Light worsted (DK)	12–15
#5 Worsted (aran)	8–12
#6 Bulky (chunky)	6–9
#7 Super bulky (super chunky)	5–6
#8 Jumbo (ultra roving)	1–4

HAND WIND A CENTER-PULL YARN BALL

Working from a center-pull skein or ball is generally smoother and faster. You don't have to constantly tug at the yarn nor have your yarn rolling all around. When time comes to wind your own ball, did you know you can make it a center-pull without any special tools? All you need are your hands.

Instructions

1. Drape the yarn over your hand, leaving a 5–6in (12.5–15cm) end (A).

2. Holding on to the yarn end, wrap the yarn around your thumb and index finger, in a figure 8 fashion (B).

3. Continue wrapping 15 to 20 more times (C, D).

4. Pinch your thumb and index finger together and slide the stack off (E, F).

5. Wrap the yarn around the stack, while continuously rotating it in the same direction. Make sure your thumb always stays on top of the stack (G, H, I).

! IMPORTANT

Do not remove your thumb from the top of the stack. Do not lose the yarn end.

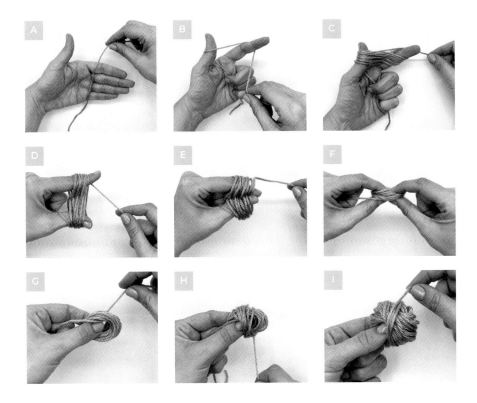

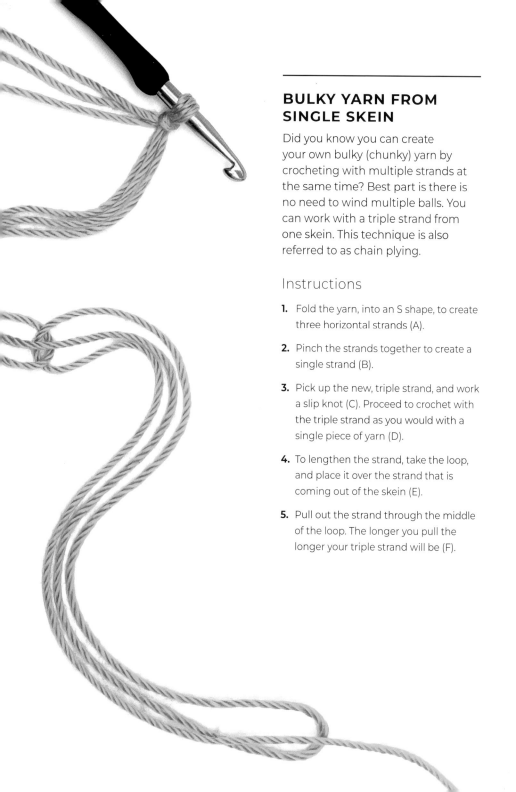

BULKY YARN FROM SINGLE SKEIN

Did you know you can create your own bulky (chunky) yarn by crocheting with multiple strands at the same time? Best part is there is no need to wind multiple balls. You can work with a triple strand from one skein. This technique is also referred to as chain plying.

Instructions

1. Fold the yarn, into an S shape, to create three horizontal strands (A).

2. Pinch the strands together to create a single strand (B).

3. Pick up the new, triple strand, and work a slip knot (C). Proceed to crochet with the triple strand as you would with a single piece of yarn (D).

4. To lengthen the strand, take the loop, and place it over the strand that is coming out of the skein (E).

5. Pull out the strand through the middle of the loop. The longer you pull the longer your triple strand will be (F).

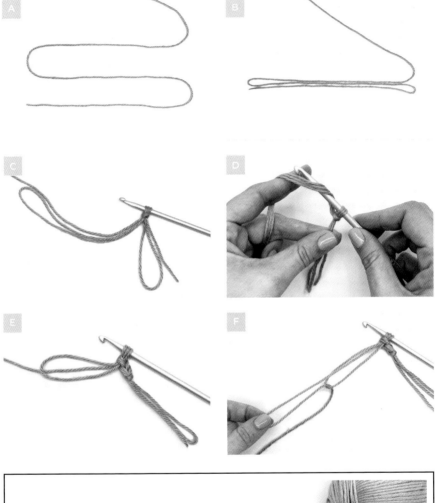

DOUBLE STRAND FROM SINGLE SKEIN

———

You can crochet double stranded from a single skein by simply pulling from the center and the outside of the skein at the same time.

NOTIONS & TOOLS

In addition to yarn and hooks you should have a variety of essential notions and tools including needles, stitch markers, scissors, and more. This section outlines some of the other supplies that are helpful to keep on hand.

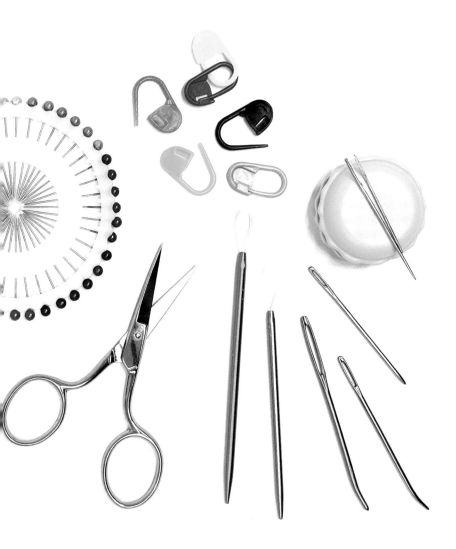

NEEDLES

Needles come in a variety of materials, shapes, and sizes. Picking the right needle for the job can be as important as picking the right hook. Here's a list of some must-have needles to keep.

Yarn needles

Yarn needles come in a variety of materials from metal to plastic. They have a large eye and a blunt point, which helps glide through stitches without splitting the yarn. They come as straight or bent tip, in a wide range of sizes.

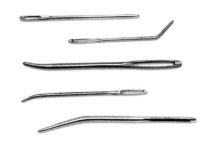

Embroidery needles

Smaller than yarn needles, embroidery needles have a long eye and a sharp point, which is perfect to use with crochet thread or for embroidering precise details on amigurumi.

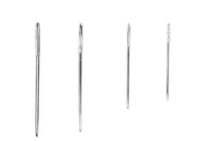

Wool and finishing needles

These flexible needles with an extra large eye are perfect for bulky (chunky) and jumbo (ultra roving) size yarns.

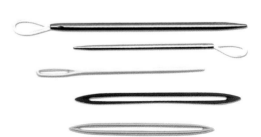

THREADING THREE WAYS

If you don't have a needle threader handy, you can use couple of common, everyday items that can be found around the house. These three simple, yet effective hacks will help you thread the needle like a pro!

The paper method

Instructions

1. Cut a strip of paper about 1–2in (2.5–5cm) long and a little less wide than the eye of the needle.

2. Fold the strip in half and place around the end of the yarn (A).

3. Feed the folded end of the paper through the eye of the needle. Pull all the way through and remove the paper (B, C, D).

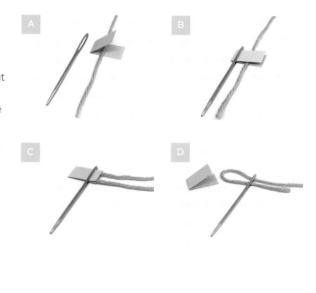

The thread method

Instructions

1. Fold a piece of thread in half and feed the ends through the eye of the needle, creating a loop (A).

2. Feed the yarn through the loop (B).

3. Pull on the ends of the thread to draw the yarn through the eye of the needle (C, D).

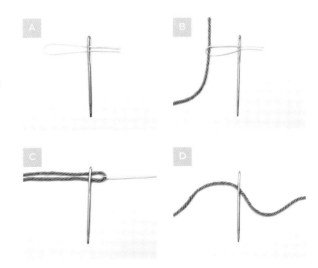

The pinch method

Instructions

1. Wrap yarn around the point of the needle and pinch, as close to the needle as possible (A).

2. Remove the needle from the loop (B).

3. Wiggle the folded end through the eye of the needle to thread it (C, D).

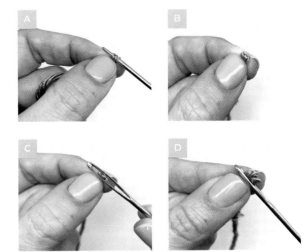

STITCH MARKERS

Stitch markers are invaluable for keeping track of rounds/rows, marking stitches, and keeping count. Stitch markers come in all shape and sizes. From the basic plastic markers, to elaborate handmade charms, the options are endless.

Basic stitch markers

Made from plastic, these basic stitch markers come in two main styles: split ring and interlocking.

Handmade stitch markers

These come in a huge variety of sizes, shapes, and materials. However, the clasps themselves come in two main styles: a lobster clasp and lever back closure.

Everything else

There are many other, everyday items that can be used as stitch markers. Safety pins, paper clips, earrings, even a scrap piece of yarn can be used as a stitch marker.

> **! IMPORTANT**
>
> *Remember that crochet stitch markers must have an opening unlike their knit counterparts, which are typically closed loops. Because crochet stitch markers are hooked directly onto the stitch, they need to be removable. Do not mix up the two!*

OTHER TOOLS & SUPPLIES

Besides all the basic notions, here are some other tools that it would be helpful to have on hand.

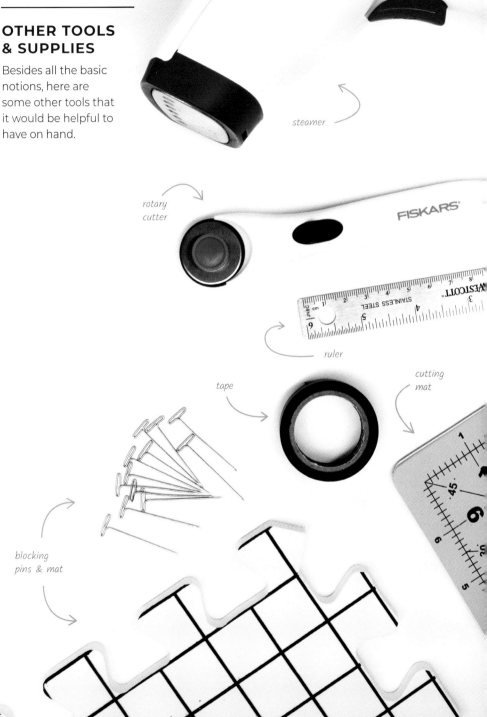

steamer

rotary cutter

ruler

tape

cutting mat

blocking pins & mat

TYING
THE KNOTS

FROM STARTING TO JOINING: TIPS AND
TRICKS ON MAKING THE PERFECT KNOT

STARTING KNOTS

One of the first steps in crochet is creating a slip knot. Although it's a simple knot, some knot-making methods make it overly complicated or hard to remember. Here are a couple of easy-to-remember ways to make a quick and easy slip knot.

SLIP KNOT WITHOUT A HOOK

Instructions

1. Wrap the yarn around the index finger, twice, going clockwise (A).

2. Slide the left loop over the right loop (B).

3. Slide the new left loop over the right loop (C) and off the finger (D).

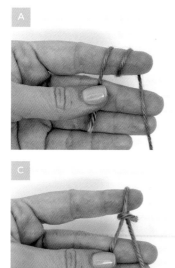

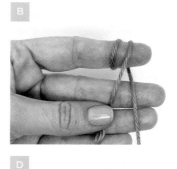

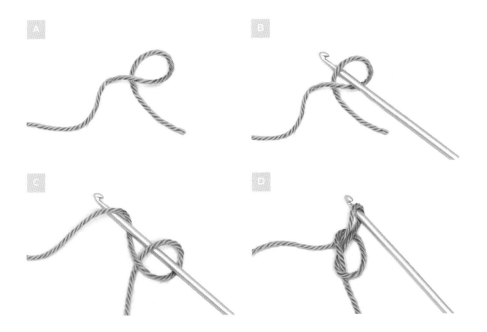

SLIP KNOT WITH A HOOK

Instructions

1. Make a loop by placing the working yarn over the yarn end (A).

2. Insert the hook into the loop (B).

3. Yarn over with the working yarn (C).

4. Draw through the loop and tighten (D).

JOINING KNOTS

There are many different methods you can use to join two pieces of yarn together. Some are more secure but leave a more visible knot, while others require a bit more finesse resulting in a more seamless join. Select the method that works best for your project. If making amigurumi, a noticeable knot might not be an issue as it can be easily hidden on the inside. Meanwhile, a lacy scarf might require a less visible join that won't show on either side.

THE MAGIC KNOT

This is one of the most secure ways to join yarn (excluding silky yarns). It's simple to make resulting in a small knot that is easy to hide.

Instructions

1. Place both ends of yarn parallel to one another, facing in the opposite direction (A).

2. Wrap the top strand over and under the bottom strand, to make a simple knot (B).

3. Wrap the bottom strand over then under the top strand and make a simple knot (C, D).

4. Pull on the ends to slide the knots together and tighten (E, F).

5. Trim the ends.

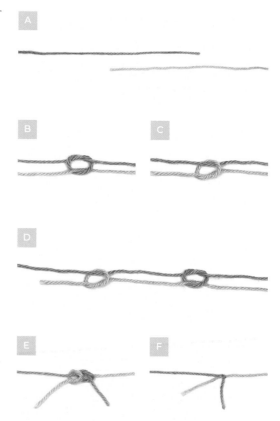

WEAVER'S KNOT

Another great knot to use for joining yarn is the weaver's knot. This method "creates" a knot with a smooth profile that will be easy to hide and will not slip. Plus, the ends can be woven in afterwards, for extra security.

Instructions

1. Begin by making a slip knot with one of the yarn ends.

2. Thread the second piece of yarn through the slip knot loop (A).

3. Grab both ends of the slip knot, and slowly begin pulling them apart (B).

4. Stop pulling when the second piece of yarn gets pulled through.

5. Pull each end of the working yarn to tighten the knot (C).

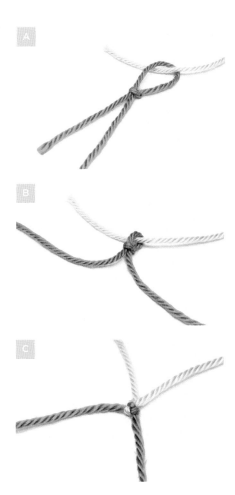

EXTRA SECURITY

If you're making an item that will be handled quite a bit, I recommend leaving quite long ends and weaving them in to make sure your finished piece won't unravel.

INVISIBLE NEEDLE JOIN

Although a bit more time consuming, this join creates a seamless and smooth transition from one color to the next without any visible knots or bumps. At the same time, the interlocking threads also make this an extremely secure joining method.

Instructions

1. Interlock two pieces of yarn as shown (A).

2. Thread one of the ends using a sharp needle.

3. Insert the needle directly through the center of that same yarn, weaving it into itself for 1–2in (2.5–5cm) (B, C).

4. Repeat the same with the other end (D).

5. Pull on each end to even out any bunching, and tighten.

6. Trim off any excess ends.

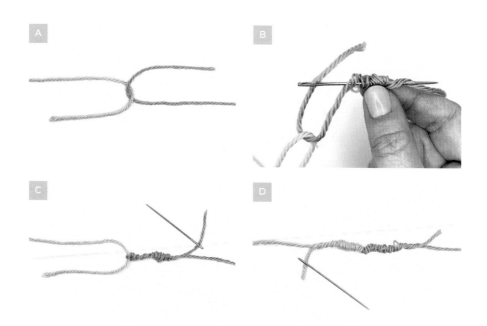

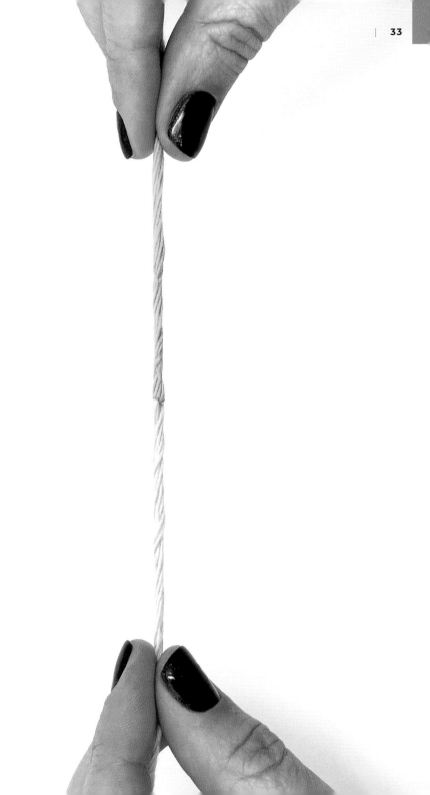

CRACKIN'
THE FOUNDATION

CHAINS, CORDS, AND STITCHES:
ALL THE TIPS AND TRICKS FOR
BUILDING A STRONG FOUNDATION

ALL ABOUT THE CHAIN

Foundation chain is a series of chain stitches that are used as the base for almost all crochet projects. It's used as a base for flat projects worked in turning rows and as a starting point for oblong and oval shaped projects worked in the round. It can even be joined together to create a base for tube shaped items.

The chain is very versatile and might be the easiest stitch to master—however, it comes with its own set of issues. Chains are flimsy, hard to work into, they twist, they bite... Well, maybe not that last part. Here are some things you can do to eliminate a few common frustrations when working the foundation chain.

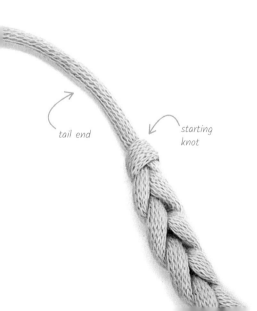

tail end

starting knot

GET THE KINKS OUT

If your chain ends up looking a little kinky, tug at both ends a couple of times—this should help even it out.

working
loop

first chain
from the hook

second chain
from the hook

working
yarn

back
loops

front
loops

back
bumps

KNOT-LESS START

Every foundation starts with a slip knot, or does it? What if I told you there was a way you can make your foundation without a visible knot? Yes, it's true, you can start your work without a bulky knot.

Instructions

1. Place the yarn end under the working yarn, to create a loop. Insert the hook inside the loop (A).

2. Pinch and hold the bottom of the loop, where two strands intersect, to keep the loop together (B).

3. Grab the working yarn and draw through the loop. This stitch will count as your first chain stitch (C, D).

4. Continue to make the rest of your chain stitches as you normally would (E, F).

5. If your first chain ends up being too big, you may gently pull on the end to tighten it. However, be careful not to pull too hard otherwise your chain will turn into a slip knot.

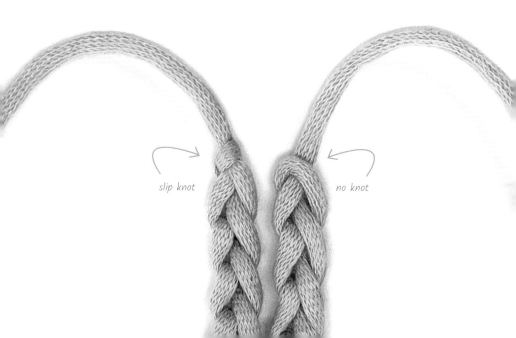

slip knot   no knot

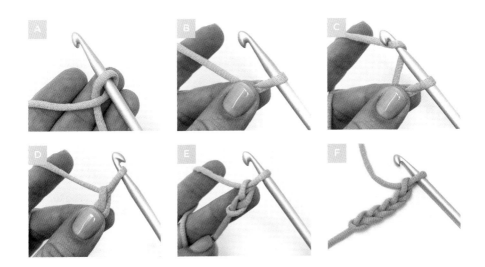

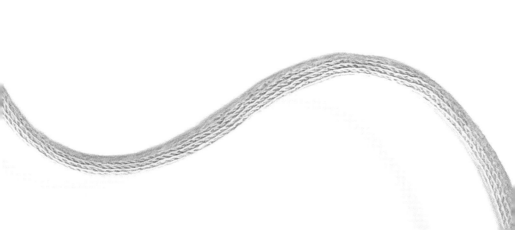

NO MORE TWISTED CHAINS

If you've ever needed to join a long foundation chain to work in the round, you know how tricky it can be. No matter how hard you try to keep everything aligned you inevitably end up with a twisted chain. The worst part is, you don't usually realize it until you've already completed the first row. However, there is a foolproof way to make sure your joining chains never twist again!

Instructions

1. Make a slip knot and begin your foundation chain as usual.

2. After working several chains, remove the hook from the working loop and insert it through the very first chain stitch, from the back to the front (A).

3. Re-insert the hook back into the working loop (B) and complete the foundation chain (C).

4. When you're ready to join, simply pull the working loop through the first stitch (D).

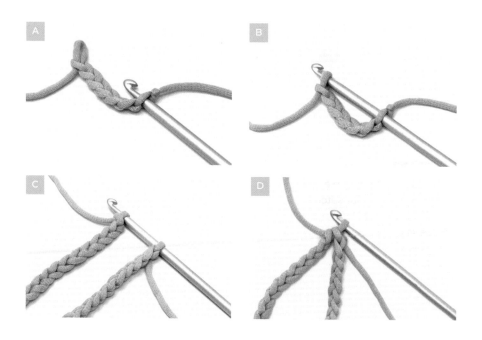

WORKING THE BACK BUMP

When working into a foundation chain, place your stitches into the back bumps instead of the chain loops. This will create a stronger and nicer looking edge (see Perfecting the Rows: Working Into the Back Bumps).

DIDN'T MAKE ENOUGH CHAINS?

It can be frustrating to get through the first row of your project only to realize your count was off and you didn't make enough chains. Usually, you would have to rip everything out and start over. However, there's a way to adjust your foundation without starting over.

To add stitches to your foundation simply work a foundation stitch into the last chain. This technique can be done with single crochet, half double crochet, and double crochet stitches—adding double crochet stitches is explained here, but it's the same technique for the other stitches (see Cracking the Foundation: Foundation Stitches).

MORE IS BETTER

When in doubt, work more chains than you might need. Once you finish working the first row of your pattern you can undo the starting knot and unravel the extra chains.

↑
*starting
foundation chain*

↑
*new
foundation stitches*

Adding double crochet (DC) stitches

Instructions

1. Turn the work 90 degrees clockwise. You will be working into the last chain of the foundation (A).

2. Yarn over, insert the hook into the last chain stitch of your foundation (B).

3. Yarn over and draw through the stitch, leaving three loops on the hook (C).

4. Yarn over and draw through the first loop only. This chain stitch will become your new foundation chain stitch (place a stitch marker into this chain) (D).

5. Yarn over and draw through two loops only, leaving two loops on the hook (E). Yarn over again and draw through both loops to finish the stitch (F).

6. To make the next stitch repeat Steps 2 to 5, placing the hook into the new foundation chain stitch (the one with the stitch marker).

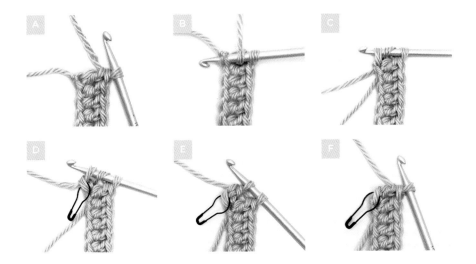

CHAINLESS FOUNDATION

Sometimes working into a foundation chain can be tricky and frustrating. Foundation chain might be the "standard" way of starting a project, but it is not the only way. Here are some chain alternatives that you may find helpful.

FOUNDATION CORD

This method replaces the chain with an i-cord, which creates a stronger foundation for working your stitches. The cord has more stretch than a traditional chain, giving your work a more flexible edge.

Instructions

1. Make a slip knot, leaving an end approximately three to four times the length of your desired foundation (A).

2. Wrap one of the yarn ends over the hook, front to back, leaving two loops on the hook (B).

3. Grab the other yarn end and draw through both loops (C, D).

4. Repeat Steps 2 and 3 until your foundation is the desired length.

5. Turn your cord 90 degrees clockwise. It might seem more intuitive to turn your work the other way, but this way you'll get a nicer looking edge.

6. Work a turning chain (see: Perfecting the Rows: Turning Chains) and proceed to crochet your first row into the cord (E, F).

*foundation
single crochet*

*foundation
half double crochet*

*foundation
double crochet*

*foundation
treble crochet*

FOUNDATION STITCHES

Foundation stitches are another alternative to a foundation chain. These magical stitches allow you to create your foundation chain and the first row of stitches simultaneously, completely eliminating the need for a chain.

Compared to a foundation chain, which has a tendency to curl, foundation stitches are much easier to keep flat. They also have more flexibility, making this foundation method ideal for garments and wearables.

Foundation stitches can be used any time your foundation row calls for basic stitches such as single crochet, half double crochet, double crochet, and so on.

Instead of working horizontally, as with the traditional chain, the foundation stitches are worked vertically, with chains stacked on top of one another.

To replace a foundation chain with foundation stitches, make sure your foundation stitch count is the same as the required stitch count for your first row.

Bear in mind, foundation stitches may not be suitable for every project. If the foundation row includes skipped, slipped, or any special stitches, this method will not work.

Foundation single crochet (FSC)

Instructions

1. Chain 2 (A).

2. Insert the hook under both loops of the first chain, draw up a loop leaving two loops on the hook (B).

3. Yarn over, draw through the first loop only (C). This creates the next foundation chain stitch (optional: place a stitch marker into this chain stitch).

4. Yarn over and draw through both loops on the hook, so that only one loop remains. This completes the first foundation stitch (D).

5. To make the next FSC, place the hook into the chain stitch created in Step 3, where you placed the stitch marker, draw up a loop (E), then repeat Steps 3 to 5 until the foundation is the desired length (F).

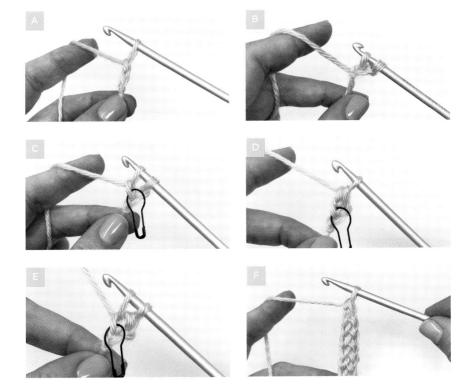

Foundation half double crochet (FHDC)

Instructions

1. Chain 2 (A).

2. Yarn over, insert the hook under both loops of the first chain and draw up a loop leaving three loops on the hook (B).

3. Yarn over, draw through the first loop only (C). This creates the foundation chain stitch (optional: place a stitch marker into this chain stitch).

4. Now complete a HDC as usual. Yarn over and draw through all three loops on the hook. This completes the first foundation half double crochet stitch (D).

5. To make the next FHDC, yarn over then place hook into the chain stitch created in Step 3, where you placed the stitch marker (E, F).

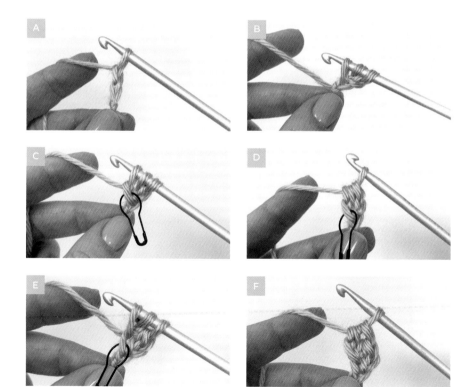

Foundation double crochet (FDC)

Instructions

1. Chain 3 (A).

2. Yarn over, insert the hook under both loops of the first chain and draw up a loop, leaving three loops on the hook (B).

3. Yarn over, draw through the first loop only (C). This creates the foundation chain stitch (optional: place a stitch marker into this chain stitch).

4. Now complete your DC as usual. Yarn over, draw through two loops on hook, yarn over, draw through the remaining two loops. This completes the first foundation half double crochet stitch (D, E).

5. To make the next FDC, yarn over then place the hook into the chain stitch created in Step 3, where you placed the stitch marker (F).

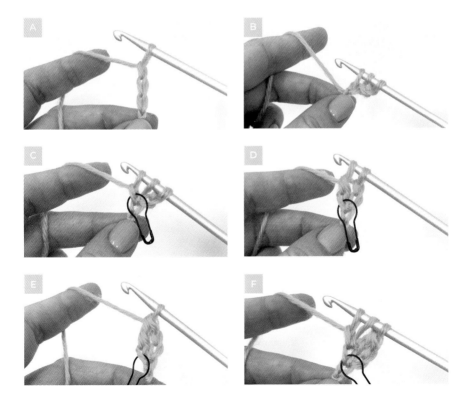

PERFECTING
THE ROWS

TIPS ON KEEPING STRAIGHT EDGES AND SMOOTH
SIDES WHEN WORKING IN TURNING ROWS

KEEPING IT EVEN

No matter how long you've been crocheting you have, more than likely, encountered your fair share of curled edges and slanting sides. Whether it's tension (gauge), hook size, or something else, the reason might not always be obvious. Learn to identify the most common of these issues and how to prevent them from happening in the future.

CURLING CORNERS

If the edges of your work are curling and your work no longer lays flat, chances are it's because of uneven tension. Tighter stitches will cause your crochet to become stiff, forcing the edges to curl.

THE FIX: Try to crochet with a looser tension, and keep it even throughout the entire project.

SLANTING SIDES

Uneven edges in crochet can often be attributed to one common mistake: incorrect stitch count. Somewhere along the line you've either added or skipped a stitch.

THE FIX: Use stitch markers to keep track of first and last stitches.

CURVING FOUNDATION

If the foundation edge of the work is curving in, it's most likely because the foundation chain is too tight. Adding stitches to a tight foundation chain will cause it to curl and bend making your work appear uneven.

THE FIX: Use a larger hook when making your foundation chain. After crocheting the chain switch back to the recommended hook size.

STITCHES THAT CURL

Some stitches simply have a natural tendency to curl—no matter what you do to try and avoid it, the edges end up curling. Don't worry you're not doing anything wrong.

THE FIX: Blocking (see Flawless Finish: Blocking Simplified) will loosen up the fibers allowing the stitches to stretch, relax, and flatten out.

WORKING INTO THE BACK BUMPS

Ever notice how the bottom edge of your work never looks quite as finished as the top? It oftentimes appears flimsy, with noticeable gaps between the foundation and the first row, and you never see those pretty V stitches, like the top of the row.

To not only make the bottom edge match the top, but also give stability to the chain, work the first row of stitches into the back bumps (see Crackin' the Foundation: All About the Chain) of the foundation chain (A).

A MUST FOR WORKING AROUND THE CHAIN

Working into the back bumps of the foundation chain makes crocheting around the chain a billion times easier. Try this technique next time you're working on an oval.

creates a clean and
secure bottom edge

TURNING CHAINS

Turning chains are typically worked between each row. Their purpose is to bring the yarn to the next row of crochet while maintaining the correct height needed to work the first stitch. Since some stitches are taller than others the number of required chains will change from stitch to stitch. Working the correct number of turning chains is also key for maintaining straight edges in your crochet. The height of the turning chain should align with the height of the stitches, ensuring your sides remain even.

single crochet

half double crochet

double crochet

treble crochet

HOW MANY CHAINS?

The length of the turning chain depends on the height of the stitch. Tall stitches require more chains while shorter stitches require fewer.

Here are some suggestions for how many chains you will need for some of the basic crochet stitches. Please note these are merely suggestions. Depending on your crochet style and tension (gauge) you might need to adjust the number of chains.

NUMBER OF TURNING CHAINS

Stitch type	Number of chains
Single crochet	1 ch
Half double crochet	2 ch
Double crochet	3 ch
Treble crochet	4 ch

DON'T COUNT THE CHAINS

Should you count the turning chain as a stitch or not? When the turning chain counts as a stitch, it replaces the very first stitch of the row. Since it is not placed directly into the first stitch, it creates a visible gap on the edges of your work.

Patterns generally specify whether turning chains count or not. However, I prefer not to count them to avoid having those gaps.

If you do not wish to count the turning chain, place the first stitch into the same space at the base of the turning chain. When you come to the end of the row, ignore the turning chain and crochet into the last stitch of the row.

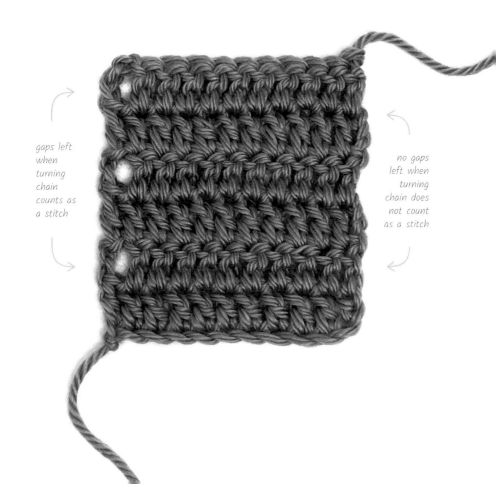

gaps left when turning chain counts as a stitch

no gaps left when turning chain does not count as a stitch

SMOOTH SIDE EDGES

Ever notice how the sides of turning rows always have a slight zig-zag look, even when they have the correct number of turning chains? Although that's just the nature of those stitches there are a couple of things you can do to eliminate the wavy edges, no matter if you're working with single, half double, double, or treble crochet.

CHAINLESS SINGLE CROCHET

One of the easiest ways to get a smoother side edge when working with single crochet is to skip the turning chain completely.

Instructions

1. After working last stitch of the row, remove the hook from the working loop (A).

2. Turn the work, then re-insert the hook back into the working loop. Do NOT chain.

3. Pull up the working loop slightly so it's approximately the same height as the height of a single crochet stitch (B).

4. Insert hook into the first stitch and make a single crochet (C).

5. Crochet the remainder of the row as usual.

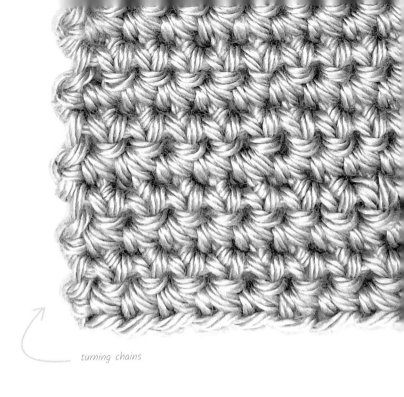

turning chains

chainless single crochet

FRONT LOOP / CHAIN LOOP TRICK

There's another method that allows you to get a smoother side edge, and this one might be my favorite. This method does not replace the chain; the difference is in how you work the very last stitch of the row. This method works well with not only a half double crochet stitch, but also a single crochet.

Single crochet (SC)

Instructions

1. Turn, chain 1, and work a new row of single crochet stitches up to the last stitch (A).

2. On the last stitch, insert the hook into the front loop only of the last stitch.

3. Then, insert the hook into the horizontal bar formed by the turning chain from the previous row (B, C).

4. Make a single crochet (D).

Half-double crochet (HDC)

Instructions

1. Chain 2, and work a new row of half double crochet stitches up to the last stitch (A).

2. On the last stitch, yarn over, insert the hook into the front loop only of the last stitch (B).

3. Then, insert the hook into the horizontal bar formed by the turning chain from the previous row (C).

4. Complete the half double crochet (D).

turning chains

stacked stitches

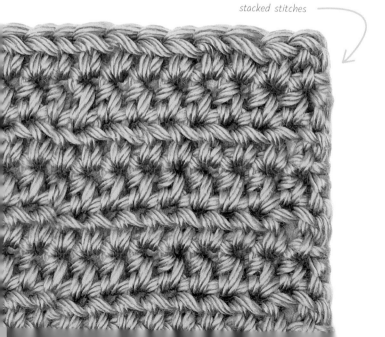

STACKED STITCHES

When working with taller stitches such as half double crochet, double crochet, and up, a great way to keep the edges smooth is to use a stacked single crochet stitch. As with a turning chain, the taller the stitch the more single crochet stitches you will have to stack on top of one another.

Instructions

1. Do not chain, place a single crochet into the first stitch of the row (A).

2. Insert the hook into the left vertical bar of the last single crochet and make another single crochet (B, C, D).

3. The two stacked single crochet stitches will replace the first half double crochet.

NUMBER OF SC STITCHES TO STACK

Stitch type	Number of stitches
Half double crochet	2 sts
Double crochet	3 sts
Treble crochet	4 sts
Double treble crochet	5 sts

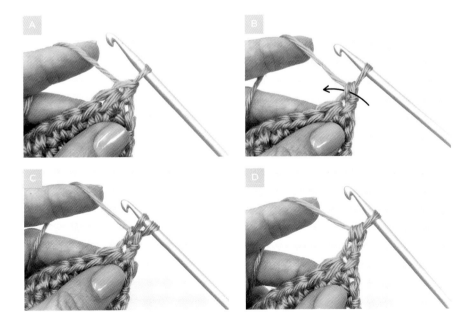

turning chains

STANDING STITCHES

Another great method of getting a nice and even side edge, when working with double crochet stitches, is to replace your turning chain and first stitch with a standing double crochet stitch.

Instructions

1. Pull up a loop approximately as tall your double crochet stitch.

2. Holding the loop against the hook with your index finger, rotate the hook around the loop, counterclockwise (A, B). Do not remove finger off the loop.

3. Insert the hook into the first stitch, yarn over with the working yarn and draw through. It will appear as if you have three loops on the hook (C).

4. Yarn over and draw through two loops on the hook (D). You may remove the finger off the loop.

5. Yarn over and draw through the remaining loops (E).

standing stitches

REFINING
THE ROUNDS

FROM RINGS TO SEAMS AND EVERYTHING
IN BETWEEN: TIPS ON KEEPING YOUR
ROUNDS PERFECT EVERY TIME

THE RINGS

Almost all projects that are worked in the round start with a ring. You can either make a chain ring (foundation ring) or a magic ring (magic circle) but have you ever wondered what the difference is? Although both methods yield similar results, they have their pros and cons.

MAGIC RING

Sometimes referred to as a magic circle, this is made by creating a loop which can be closed completely. This method is used mainly in amigurumi or for decorative crochet pieces.

Pros

- Can be pulled completely closed
- Creates a slimmer foundation
- Has a more seamless look

Cons

- Can be tricky to master
- Not recommended with silky yarns

CHAIN RING

Also known as a foundation ring, this is made by working a series of chains and joining them together to form a circle. This method is commonly used for items that will see a lot of use, such as blankets and garments.

Pros

- Simple to make
- Very secure
- Works with silky/slippery yarns

Cons

- Leaves a hole in the center
- Has more bulk than a magic ring

CLOSING A CHAIN RING

Although a chain ring cannot be completely closed on its own you can use the yarn end to close it up. After completing the first round weave the tail through the base of all the stitches, then pull to close (A, B).

EXTRA SECURE MAGIC RING

One of the biggest negatives of a magic ring is that, depending on how they are made, they can easily unravel. To avoid any future disasters I recommend making a double loop, which makes your magic ring extra secure.

Instructions

1. Place the yarn over your index finger and wrap twice around the middle finger (A).

2. Insert the hook through both loops on the middle finger and grab the working yarn (B).

3. Draw the working yarn through both loops (C).

4. Work a chain stitch to secure (D). This completes the magic ring.

5. Add the first round of stitches into the ring.

6. To close the ring first pull on the loop that is coming out of the same space as the end. This will cinch the other loop (E).

7. Pull on the yarn end to close the ring completely (F).

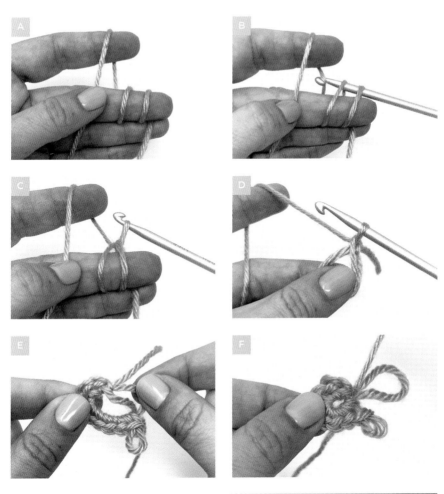

LEAVE IT ON!

Leave the ring on your finger when placing the first few stitches into the ring. This especially helps when adding many stitches because it keeps the ring wide and open.

ALL ABOUT THE ROUNDS

There are three basic methods to crocheting a circle—yes, I said three! You might be thinking of two: continuous rounds (spiral) and joining rounds. But there's also a third, turning rounds. While one method is more commonly used for amigurumi, another method is used for colorwork and garments. What is the difference and when should you use them?

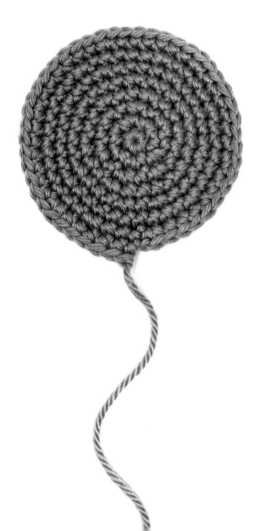

SPIRAL ROUNDS

Spiral rounds are worked continuously, without slip stitching or chaining. This creates a perfect surface without any visible seams. However, because of the nature of a spiral, the rounds never truly connect with the stitches always stacked at a slight angle. Continuous rounds also make it difficult to tell where each round starts and stops.

Spiral rounds are most often used in amigurumi.

USE A STITCH MARKER

When working in continuous spiral rounds, use a stitch marker to keep track of where your round starts/ends.

JOINING ROUNDS

This method is worked in distinct rounds that are joined at the end. The stitches stack perfectly on top of one another and make it clear where each round starts and ends, even without stitch markers. The negative of this method is that it results in visible seams that can be tricky to hide (see Tackling the Seams).

Joining rounds are often used in garments and colorwork.

TURNING ROUNDS

Technically this is also a joined round, however, instead of working in the same direction, you turn after each round like you do when crocheting in rows. Some stitches look completely different when worked in the same direction or turned, so it's important to know if your pattern requires turning rounds or not.

Turning rounds are most often used in garments and granny squares.

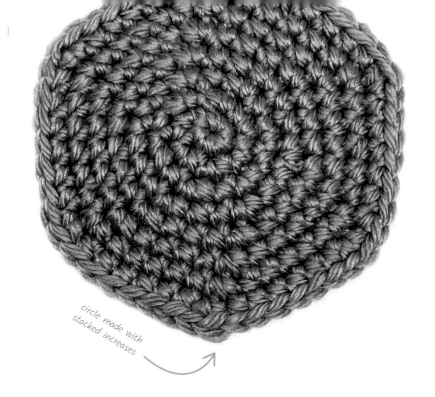

circle made with
stacked increases

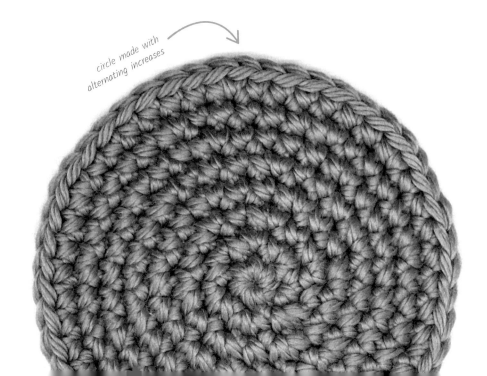

circle made with
alternating increases

PERFECTLY ROUND CIRCLE

Ever notice how sometimes circles don't quite look like circles, but more like hexagons? Don't worry, you're not doing anything wrong. It's because of how patterns are written. They basically force us to make hexagons by telling us to stack all of the increases on top of one another.

A simple trick to make sure that circles always come out looking round is to alternate the placement of the increases. There are many ways in which you can do so, but the main way is to alternate them in even or odd rounds.

Stacked increases

Make a magic ring.

Round 1: 6sc.

Round 2: [**Inc**] 6 times.

Round 3: [**Inc**, 1sc] 6 times.

Round 4: [**Inc**, 2sc] 6 times.

Round 5: [**Inc**, 3sc] 6 times.

Round 6: [**Inc**, 4sc] 6 times.

Round 7: [**Inc**, 5sc] 6 times.

Round 8: [**Inc**, 6sc] 6 times.

Alternating increases

Make a magic ring.

Round 1: 6sc.

Round 2: [**Inc**] 6 times.

Round 3: [**Inc**, 1sc] 6 times.

Round 4: [1sc, **inc**, 1sc] 6 times.

Round 5: [**Inc**, 3sc] 6 times.

Round 6: [2sc, **inc**, 2sc] 6 times.

Round 7: [**Inc**, 5sc] 6 times.

Round 8: [3sc, **inc**, 3sc] 6 times.

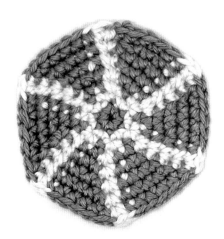
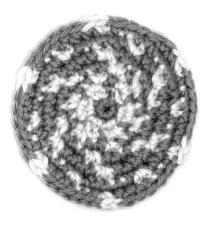

single crochet

half double crochet

double crochet

treble crochet

PERFECTLY FLAT CIRCLE

Getting your circle to be perfectly flat can be as tricky as getting it perfectly round. The biggest culprit that keeps your circle from laying flat is the stitch count. Starting with the correct number of stitches is key, but what is that number exactly?

Most books, blogs, and tutorials will give you a specific, standard number, but crochet is not an exact science. Other variables, from tension (gauge) to hook size, play a part in shaping your final piece, so the same stitch count might not work for everyone.

If you find your circle won't lay flat when using the standard number of starting stitches, try increasing the stitch count.

For a guide to the recommended range of starting stitches for each basic crochet stitch, see the table.

NUMBER OF STITCHES TO ADD IN ROUND 1

Stitch type	Number of stitches
Single crochet	6–8 sts
Half double crochet	8–10 sts
Double crochet	10–12 sts
Treble crochet	12–14 sts

Once you have the right number of starting stitches it's important to make sure you always increase by the correct amount. Count the stitches after each round to make sure you always have the correct stitch count.

Curling edges

If the edges of your circle are curling inward, chances are you didn't work enough increases. Re-count your stitches to see where you might have missed an increase.

Rippling edges

If your circle is rippling and the edges look like a wave then you might have added too many stitches to your work. Re-count your stitches to find our where the extras were placed. Frog (unravel) the incorrect round/s and re-do.

TACKLING THE SEAMS

Whether you're working a flat circle or a tube, the most frustrating part about working in joining rounds is the seams. Not only are they quite noticeable but they also have a tendency to slant. Wish there was something you can do to even them out? Better yet, something to hide them completely? I've got you covered!

PREVENT THE SLANT

Crocheting in joining rounds typically results in a diagonal seam no matter what stitch you're working with. The taller the stitch the more noticeable the slant. This happens due to the nature of crochet stitches. The base of the stitch sits directly on top of the stitch below. The top of that stitch, however, gets pushed slightly to the side.

There are two simple ways you can prevent the slant and keep it straight, it just depends on whether you are working in turning rounds or not.

turning method

Method #1—Turning

The easiest way to fix this is to work in turning rounds, meaning that you turn your work before working the next round just as you do when working in rows. Although this technique will surely straighten out that seam, it only works for projects where turning is OK.

alternating method

Method #2—Alternating

When working without turning you can straighten the seam by alternating the placement of the first stitch. Typically a pattern will note whether to place the first stitch into the "next stitch" or into the "same stitch as chain" but with this method you do both.

Instructions

For every odd round place the first stitch into the same stitch as the turning chain (A). For every even round place it into the next stitch (B).

INVISIBLE SEAM WITH SINGLE CROCHET

Now that we've tackled making seams straight let's try to make them less visible. There are a few methods to hide a seam, depending on the stitch you're working with. If working with single crochet joining rounds here's how you would keep those seams less visible.

Instructions

1. Work to the end of the round (A).

2. Remove the hook from the working loop and insert it into the joining stitch, placing it back to front (B).

3. Place the working loop over the hook and draw the loop through the stitch (C, D).

4. Chain 1.

5. Insert the hook back into the same joining stitch and work a single crochet. This will be the first stitch in the next round (E, F).

visible chain seam

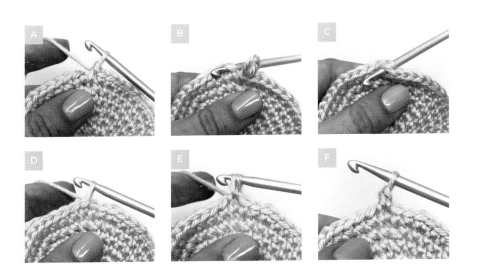

invisible single crochet seam

INVISIBLE SEAM WITH STACKED STITCHES

Stacked stitches aren't just great for smoothing out the edges of turning rows (see Perfecting the Rows: Smooth Side Edges—Stacked Stitches). They can also be used to hide the seam when working in joining rounds. Stack two single crochet stitches to replace a half double crochet, or stack more for taller stitches.

Instructions

1. Chain 1, then place a single crochet stitch into the first stitch of the round (A).

2. Insert the hook into the left vertical bar of the single crochet and make another single crochet (B, C, D).

3. The two stacked single crochet stitches will replace the first half double crochet stitch.

NUMBER OF SC STITCHES TO STACK

Stitch type	Number of stitches
Half double crochet	2 sts
Double crochet	3 sts
Treble crochet	4 sts
Double treble crochet	5 sts

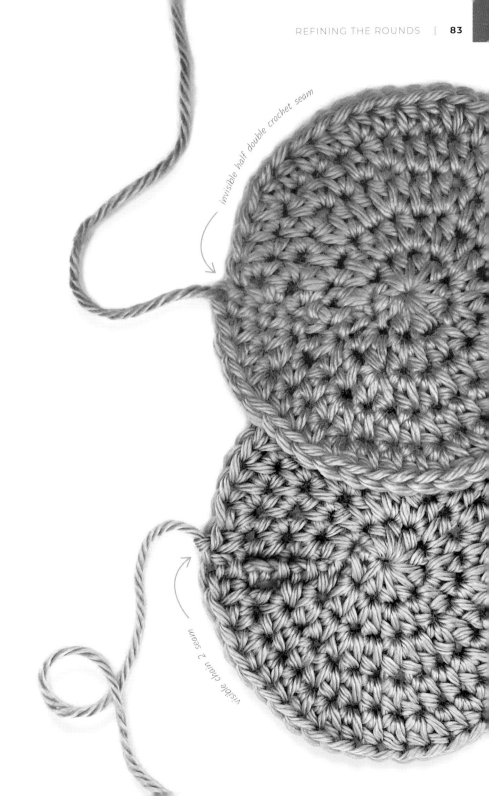

invisible half double crochet seam

visible chain 2 seam

INVISIBLE SEAM WITH DOUBLE CROCHET

When working with double crochet stitches, replace the chain with a standing double crochet stitch to make your seams barely visible. The standing stitch mimics the look of the other double crochet stitches, camouflaging the seam into the work.

Instructions

1. Pull up on the working loop so that it is approximately the height of your double crochet stitch (A).

2. Holding the loop against the hook with your finger, rotate the hook around the loop, counterclockwise (B).

3. Insert the hook into the first stitch, yarn over and draw up a loop. It will appear as if you have three loops on the hook (C). Do not remove finger off the loop.

4. Yarn over (D) and draw through two loops on the hook (E). You may now let go of the initial loop.

5. Yarn over and draw through the remaining loops to finish the stitch (F).

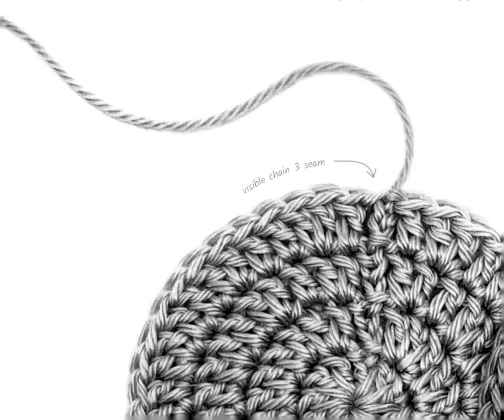

visible chain 3 seam

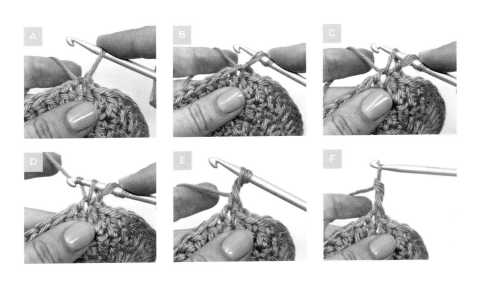

invisible double crochet seam

WORKING
WITH COLOR

BEST METHODS AND TECHNIQUES FOR PERFECT
COLOR CHANGES AND SEAMLESS COLOR JOINS

SEAMLESS COLOR CHANGE

Changing color in crochet may not be that difficult, the tricky part is making that transition as smooth as possible. Whether you're switching at the beginning or middle of the row/round, these tips can help make your color changes as seamless as they can be.

REPLACE THE CHAIN

When switching to a new color at the beginning of the row or round, the typical way is to join the new color with a slip stitch and a chain. For a more seamless way to add new color, replace the slip stitch and the chain with a standing crochet stitch so that your joining stitch will look exactly like the rest of your stitches.

Standing single crochet stitch

Instructions

1. Begin with a slip knot on your hook (A).

2. Insert the hook into the first stitch and draw up a loop (B).

3. Yarn over and draw through both loops on the hook (C).

OTHER STANDING STITCHES

To work a standing half double, double, or treble stitch, yarn over before inserting hook into the first stitch, then finish as you would a standard version of that stitch.

MID ROW COLOR CHANGE

The standard way of joining color in the middle of a row/round is to simply finish the stitch in one color then work the next stitch in a new color. However, this will cause the top V of the stitch to still appear in the old color, creating a less than perfect color change. There are two methods that can fix this. Both achieve the same thing but in a slightly different way. Give each a try and see which method you prefer. You might be surprised!

Color change method #1

Attaching the new color on the last yarn over of the previous stitch.

This method is fairly straightforward. No joining, slip stitching or chaining required. The drawbacks are that it can be tricky to get the right tension (gauge), and always remembering to switch in the previous stitch.

Instructions

1. Work the last stitch of the current color until the very last yarn over (A).

2. Yarn over with the new color and draw through all loops on the hook (B).

3. Begin working with the new color (C).

Color change method #2

This method takes an extra step, but I promise it's worth it. If you struggle with tension (gauge) in your color changes, this is the one to try. It allows you to fully complete a stitch in the old color, then work the new stitch in the new color, making sure that the top and bottom of the stitches will match.

Instructions

1. After completing the last stitch of the current color, remove the hook from the working loop and re-insert it through the top of the V and the vertical bar of the last stitch (A, B, C).

2. Grab the new color and draw through all loops on the hook (D).

3. Pull on the working yarn of the old color, to unravel the loop—don't panic, this will only unravel the loop, your work won't unravel completely, I promise (E)!

4. Proceed to work stitches with the new color (F).

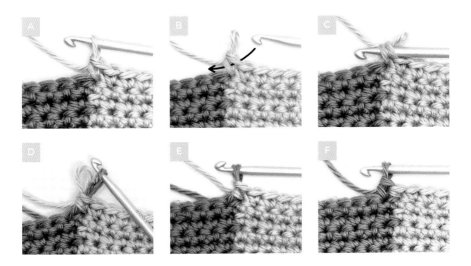

PERFECT STRIPES

Elevate your colorwork by making perfect stripes with clean edges and seamless joins.

CLEAN STRIPE

Sure, traditional color changes look fine, but sometimes you want a stripe that doesn't have those wavy edges. Clean stripes can be achieved by adding a series of slip stitches into back or front loops, depending on whether you're working in rounds or rows. Typically, the slip stitches do not count as a round or row, as they do not add much height to the stripe. However, it is important to remember that that having too many stripes will eventually add up and affect the overall size of your project.

Working in the round

Instructions

1. Attach the new color yarn and slip stitch into the back loop of all the stitches (A).

2. Single crochet into the back loops of all the slip stitches (B). Be careful not to make your slip stitches too tight.

traditional color stripe in the round

clean color stripe in the round

Working in turning rows

Instructions

1. Attach the new color yarn and slip stitch into the front loop of all the stitches (A). Turn.

2. Insert hook under the horizontal bar of previous color, and the front loop of the slip stitch, then work a standard single crochet (B, C).

SMOOTH JOINS

The trickiest part of creating color stripes while working in the round is getting them to join seamlessly. More often than not you end up with a visible jog, making one side of your work looking less than great. If you ever wondered why, and what you can do to prevent it, I have some answers.

I hate to be the bearer of bad news but if you're working in continuous rounds there's just no way to get a perfectly seamless color join. No matter what, there will always be a visible step, as that is just the nature of working in a spiral. However, there's a trick to help you eliminate the harsh step and replace it with a smoother transition.

Instructions

1. Attach the new color (see Seamless Color Change: Mid Row Color Change) (A).

2. Slip stitch into the first stitch of the new round (as tight as possible) and chain 1. This slst+ch1 combo will be replacing the first stitch of the round (B).

3. Finish crocheting the rest of the round.

4. Skip the slip stitch made in Step 2 and place the first stitch of the next round into the chain stitch 2 (C).

5. Proceed to crochet the rest of the round.

standard color join *smooth color join* *perfect color join*

THE PERFECT JOIN

Although the perfect join cannot be achieved working in continuous rounds, that does not mean that it can't be made in another way. To create a perfect color join you simply need to join the last round, then attach the new color with a standing stitch.

This method is definitely more time consuming than the previous jog-less version. But in instances where you need your stripe to be completely perfect, this comes in handy.

Instructions

1. After completing the row in the first color, break off the yarn and fasten off (see Flawless Finish: Fastening Off—Weaving In).

2. Attach the new color using the standing crochet stitch (see Seamless Color Change: Replacing the Chain).

3. Proceed to crochet the rest of your round, or work in continuous rounds without joining.

> **PRO TIP**
>
> ▬
>
> You don't have to work in joining rounds for the entire pattern, only the rounds with the color changes.

COLORWORK CLEAN-UP

The nature of crochet stitches is that they aren't perfectly symmetrical. This can be easily observed in colorwork. Often one side of the stitches doesn't quite look like the other side, which can be frustrating when you're a perfectionist. Utilizing all the tips in this section can help keep your work looking the best it can, but there's something else you can do.

COVER THE IMPERFECTIONS

To clean up your colorwork, simply cover any imperfections by stitching over them using a tapestry needle and yarn (A).

before cleaning up colorwork

after cleaning up colorwork

COLOR WITHOUT COMMITMENT

To add color to your work without the commitment of doing actual colorwork, try slip stitch surface crochet. Surface crochet involves crocheting stitches directly on top of a completed fabric, which allows you to easily change or remove the design without having to start everything over. Although surface crochet can be used with almost any basic stitch, for a variety of reasons, the slip stitch method is an especially great alternative to colorwork.

SLIP STITCH SURFACE CROCHET

Use this method to "embroider" the work by crocheting a series of linking chain stitches on top of the work. The chain stitches lay flat against the surface creating a more seamless look, which is great for adding contrasting stripes, detailed designs, or even lettering.

Instructions

1. Make a slip knot on the hook with the new color yarn.

2. Insert hook through the surface of the work between two stitches, front to back (A).

3. Draw the loop through the top of the work making sure the actual slip knot and the working yarn remain in the back of the work (B).

4. Insert the hook through the next space, between the stitches, and yarn over with the working yarn (C).

5. Draw the yarn through the top of the work (D) and through the loop on the hook, making a slip stitch (E).

6. Continue repeating Steps 4 and 5 (F).

SECRETS OF
AMIGURUMI

MUST-KNOW TIPS, TRICKS, AND TECHNIQUES
FOR TACKLING THE ART OF AMIGURUMI

AMIGURUMI ESSENTIALS

Amigurumi is the Japanese art of crocheting (or knitting) stuffed dolls and yarn creatures. Instead of flat rows, amigurumi is typically worked in the round, making 3D shapes that are stuffed and then assembled together. Although it's still crochet, making amigurumi does come with its own set of rules and best practices.

Yarn

Amigurumi can be made with virtually any yarn in any size but is commonly made with cotton or acrylic yarns in light worsted (DK) or worsted (aran) weights.

100% cotton will give your amigurumi the best stitch definition but it can be tough to work with. A cotton blend is a great alternative.

Acrylic yarn is another wonderful option because it's readily available, budget friendly, and comes in a large array of colors.

Crochet thread is great for embroidering features and details.

Hooks

Amigurumi is typically worked with tight tension (gauge) therefore steel or metal hooks are recommended.

Needles

A standard yarn needle is all that you really need, but having a bent tip needle will make your life so much easier.

Safety eyes

Typically made from plastic or glass, these pre-made eyes come in an array of sizes, styles, and colors. They usually include a plastic washer that is used to secure the eye on the inside of the crochet.

Stitch markers

Since amigurumi is typically worked in a continuous spiral, using stitch markers is a must for keeping track of your rounds.

Stuffing

Fiber fill, cotton, wool, plastic pellets, yarn scraps, or anything else soft that you can stuff inside.

Other tools & supplies

Some other things to have on hand when making amigurumi are:

- Scissors
- Craft or floral wire and jewelry pliers
- Craft glue
- Fabric felt

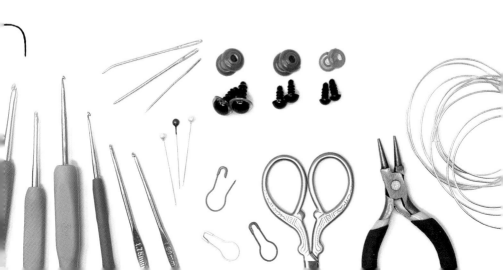

CLOSING THE GAPS

Nobody likes seeing gaps in their amigurumi. Loose tension (gauge) creates holes that allow stuffing to show through making the finished piece appear sloppy. To prevent gaps in the finished fabric, stitches must be made as tight as possible. Besides gauge, there are several other things you can do to keep those stitches really tight.

HOOK SIZE MATTERS

One of the easiest ways to avoid gaps and holes in your amigurumi is to crochet with a smaller hook. Disregard what the yarn label suggests and use a hook two or more sizes smaller than recommended. If the yarn label suggests a 5mm (H-8) hook, go down to 4mm (G-6), 3.5mm (E-4) or even 3mm (C-2 or D-3). The smaller the hook the tighter the stitches. Using a smaller hook will also result in a smaller finished size, even when using the same weight yarn. Just look at the difference in size when going from a 5mm (H-8) hook to a 3mm (C-2 or D-3) one.

SAME YARN, DIFFERENT HOOK

5mm
(US H-8)

4mm
(US G-6)

3mm
(US C-2 or D-3)

YARN UNDER

Did you know there was a difference between the way you grab your working yarn for a standard single crochet stitch when making amigurumi? The standard way is yarning over, where the yarn is placed over the hook before being drawn through the stitch.

When making amigurumi, it's best to use the yarn under technique, grabbing the yarn when it's under the hook, before drawing it through the stitch (A).

The yarn under method uses slightly less yarn, resulting in stitches that are automatically tighter than their yarn over counterparts. Similar to using a smaller hook this also results in a smaller size finished piece.

This technique creates more defined stitches resembling a letter X. This is why it is sometimes referred to as cross-stitch single crochet. The grid-like pattern created by the stitches makes an ideal surface for adding details such as embroidery.

yarn over method

yarn under method

INVISIBLE DECREASE

The standard way of decreasing, by single crocheting two stitches together, often leaves visible gaps and holes. The invisible decrease method creates tighter stitches eliminating those pesky gaps and giving your amigurumi a neater finish.

Instructions

1. Insert the hook into the front loop only of the first stitch of the decrease (A).

2. Insert the hook into the front loop only of the next stitch (B).

3. Yarn under and draw the working yarn through two loops (C).

4. Yarn over and draw through the remaining two loops to finish the stitch (D).

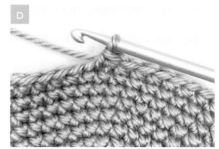

standard decrease

invisible decrease

INVISIBLE INCREASE

If you notice that your increases are also leaving gaps between stitches, try working the invisible increase instead.

Instructions

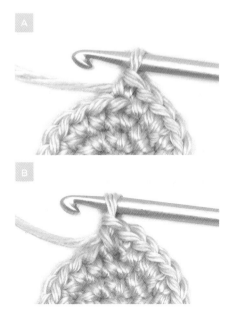

1. Place the first stitch into the back loop only of the designated increase stitch (A).

2. Place the next stitch into both loops of that same stitch (B).

THE ART OF STUFFING

Believe it or not, stuffing amigurumi is a skill in itself. Knowing how to stuff, and how much stuffing to add, can mean the difference between a perfect amigurumi and a misshapen, lumpy mess.

WHAT TO USE

The most commonly used stuffing for amigurumi is polyester fiber fill. Although other options are also available, such as wool, cotton or plastic pellets, polyester fiber fill is inexpensive and is relatively easy to find.

Yarn scraps also work great as stuffing, as long as you have enough. If you want to be a little extra careful, separate them into dark and light so that you can use the light scraps when stuffing pieces made from light yarn, and dark scraps for pieces made from dark yarn.

under-stuffed   *just right*   *over-stuffed*

HOW TO STUFF

Stuffing amigurumi with fiber fill might not seem difficult but there are certain things you can do to make sure your piece comes out perfect each time.

Instructions

- Break up the fiber fill into smaller pieces to prevent big lumps. The smaller the pieces the smoother your amigurumi will look (A).

- Use a wooden stick, or a chopstick, to push the stuffing into every nook and cranny. The stick will also help when adding stuffing through a small opening (B).

- Don't be afraid to stuff. Under-stuffing will cause the piece to look deflated and misshapen. Continue stuffing until your piece feels firm, but stop before you start seeing stuffing through the stitches.

CLEAN FINISH

Many amigurumi patterns simply tell you to "fasten off" but not many actually explain how to do it. Here are some tips to help put the finishing touches on your amigurumi.

CLOSING THE OPENING

Sure, you can continue to decrease stitches until only one is left, but there's a better method that allows you to close the final hole with a fasten off that mimics the look of the starting ring.

Instructions

1. After the last round of stitches break off the yarn, leaving 6–8in (15–20cm) end.

2. Using a needle, weave the tail through the front loops of all the stitches, from the inside out, always placing the needle in the same direction (A, B).

3. Pull on the yarn end to close the opening (C).

   NOTE:

   You may also insert the needle from the outside in, as long as you keep the same direction for all stitches.

COVERING THE GAPS

No matter how hard you try and how tight you crochet you may still end up with a couple of visible gaps. When starting over is not an option, use a yarn needle and the same yarn to cover up the holes and prevent the stuffing from showing (A, B, C).

ASSEMBLY TIPS

Assembly might be my least favorite part of amigurumi. Nevertheless the majority of amigurumi patterns require some type of sewing. Whether it's a major limb or a small detail, using these tips can help make assembly a little easier.

Leaving ends

As you finish making each part leave a yarn end after fastening off. The end can then be used to attach the pieces together.

Sewing pins

Use sewing pins to get the right placement for all the pieces and keep them from shifting when sewing them together.

Bent needle

Bent needles make it much easier to weave in and out of small stitches and 3D objects.

Using mattress stitch

If you were going to master only one stitch for assembling amigurumi, I recommend the mattress stitch—a stitch that creates a strong and virtually invisible seam. It can be used to attach two open-ended pieces together, or an open-ended piece with a closed one.

Instructions

1. Feed the needle and yarn end to the front of the work, through a stitch on one of the pieces.

2. Holding both pieces together, insert the needle around the post of a corresponding stitch on the other piece, and draw through (A, B).

3. Insert the needle back into the stitch on the other piece, through which you drew up the last yarn end, and up around the next stitch (C, D).

4. Repeat Step 3 for a few more stitches, then pull on the working end to tighten the stitches and see them disappear (E, F).

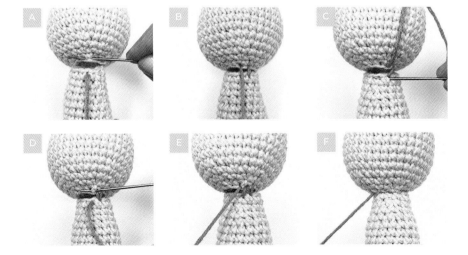

BEYOND SAFETY EYES

One of the distinct characteristics of amigurumi is the cute, kawaii style features, added to give each piece its own personality. Using safety eyes, and other pre-made features, is one of the more popular ways of doing this but definitely not the only way. Here are some other helpful and versatile methods you can use.

EMBROIDERY

Using embroidery is one of my favorite ways of adding features to amigurumi. It allows you to control the exact placement, shape, and size of the detail, making this one of the most versatile techniques. And unlike with pre-made safety eyes, these details can be added after the piece is assembled.

A straight or running stitch is great for adding simple features but if you want to take things up to the next level, try these techniques.

Wrapped stitches

Ever wonder how people embroider those perfectly smooth, curved lines that do not look like a series tiny dashes? Whether prefer using a straight stitch, running stitch or back stitch, the trick is to wrap them at the end.

Instructions

1. Use sewing pins to outline the shape and placement of the feature you're adding (the more pins you place the more detailed the line will be) (A).

2. Make a series of stitches connecting the pins (B).

3. Weave the tail end through each stitch, by placing the needle under each stitch, from bottom to top, always in the same direction (C, D).

French knot

This is the perfect stitch to use for a 3D eye, or even a nose, when making small amigurumi.

Instructions

1. Bring the needle and yarn to the front of your work, through the stitch where you would like the knot to be (A).

2. Wrap the yarn around the needle at least two to three times (the more wraps the larger the knot will be) (B).

3. Holding the wrapped yarn around the needle, as tight as you are able to, insert the tip of the needle back into the work, as close to the initial exit point as possible (C).

4. Pull the needle out through the back and tighten to form the knot on the surface (D).

> ! IMPORTANT
>
> *Do not insert the needle back into the same exact stitch/space it came out of or the knot will unravel.*

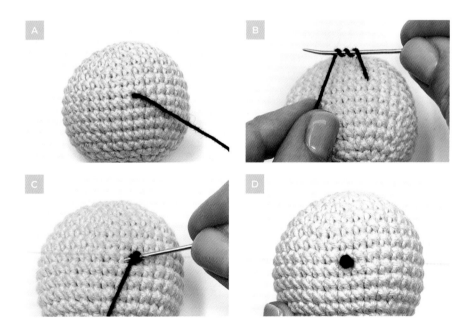

Combination embroidery

Embroidery can also be used in conjunction with pre-made features, such as safety eyes, to give more detail to your work.

Use a simple straight stitch to create eyelashes next to the safety eye. Stitch directly over part of the eye to create a top or bottom eyelid and give your amigurumi more personality.

USING MAKE-UP

Yes, you read that right, make-up! For decorative amigurumi, using pink blush or pink eyeshadow is a simple and easy way to add those cute blushing cheeks. And if you're not happy with the placement, just use make-up remover wipes and start over.

FABRIC FELT

Fabric felt (or craft felt) is a great option to consider using for adding features and details. It pairs well with crochet, can be cut to any shape and size, and can be easily attached with a fine needle and thread, or glue.

Method #1—Beyond basic

Cut out simple shapes from a single piece of felt to create eyes, mouth, cheeks, or any other feature. Or cut out several shapes from different color felt and stack together to create those kawaii style eyes, or an expressive mouth.

Method #2—Combination

Use felt in conjunction with safety eyes, by placing the stem of the safety eye directly through a piece of felt, then using scissors to trim to the desired shape (A) before attaching to the amigurumi (B).

CROCHET

For larger amigurumi, crochet features are a great alternative. They require no special tools or techniques and can either be sewn or glued to the piece, directly, after assembly.

Crochet eyes

Instructions

- These are worked in continuous rounds.

1. Using black thread: make a magic ring and add 6 single crochet stitches into the ring.

2. Using eye color thread: place 2 single crochet stitches into every stitch (A).

3. Using white thread: [place 2 single crochet stitches into one stitch, place 1 single crochet into the next] repeat until the end of the round—18 sts (B).

4. Stitch a highlight using white thread, to give the eye a little more pop (C).

Crochet cheeks

Instructions

- Make a magic ring with 6 to 8 single crochet stitches. Fasten off.

- For larger cheeks make a ring with 8 to 10 half double crochet, or 10 to 12 double crochet stitches.

EFFORTLESS
ASSEMBLY

NEED-TO-KNOW TIPS AND TECHNIQUES
FOR HASSLE-FREE CROCHET ASSEMBLY

STITCHED JOINS

Stitched joins, or seams, are made using a needle and are a simple yet effective way to attach crochet pieces together. From completely invisible to decorative, there's a stitched join for every project. Here are few seaming techniques every crocheter should know.

AVOID MESSY SEAMS

When joining pieces together, block first to even out all the edges and allow the stitches to easily align (see Flawless Finish: Blocking Simplified). Once aligned, use stitch markers to link corners and prevent the pieces from shifting during assembly.

WHIP STITCH

A simple yet versatile method of seaming flat pieces together. It's durable and fast to work up. It can be hidden on the inside of the work, or used as a decorative join on the outside edges.

Instructions

1. Place pieces together making sure the corresponding stitches are aligned on both sides. For a hidden seam the wrong sides should be facing out. For a decorative seam the right sides should be facing out.

2. Using a yarn needle and a separate piece of yarn, join by stitching through crochet stitches, always placing the needle in the same direction, back to front (A, B).

WHIP STITCH BORDER

Whip stitch can also be used as a decorative edging, without joining anything.

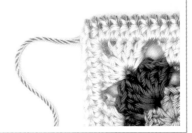

INVISIBLE SEAM STITCH

Some refer to it as mattress stitch, some call it a ladder stitch. Whatever the name, this is a great stitch to use when you want to join pieces without adding any extra detail.

Instructions

1. Hold pieces together with the right sides facing out, making sure all the corresponding stitches are aligned on both sides (A).

2. Insert needle through the top center of a stitch on one of the sides (B).

3. Pull the needle up through the bottom center of the next stitch on the same side (C).

4. Repeat Steps 2 and 3 for the corresponding stitches on the other side (D).

5. Every 5–10 stitches lay the pieces flat and pull on both ends to tighten the stitches.

NO-SEW JOINS

Don't like to sew? Using a hook is another great way to join pieces of crochet together. Some crochet seams leave a clean and almost invisible finish, while others are great for more decorative purposes. Choosing the appropriate join is an important part of your project's construction, assuring the proper shape and appearance.

FLAT SLIP STITCH JOIN

One basic but versatile crochet join is the slip stitch. However, instead of joining through both loops of the crochet stitches, this method is worked into the inside loops only. This creates a flat join, that blends right in if worked in the same color yarn, but also looks great made with a contrasting yarn.

Instructions

1. Place your squares on a flat surface, side by side, with the right sides facing upwards.

2. Insert the hook into the back loop of the square in the front (A).

3. Insert the hook into the front loop of the square in the back, placing your hook from back to front (B).

4. Yarn over and draw through all loops on the hook (C).

When crocheting over another seam, make a chain 1, then insert the hook into the inside loops of the stitches on the next two squares and proceed to join as before (D).

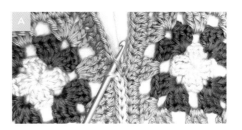

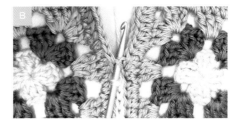

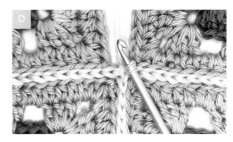

ZIG-ZAG JOIN

A zig-zag join is a variation on a flat slip stitch join. This join creates a beautiful decorative seam that is not too bulky and can lay perfectly flat.

The zig-zag pattern is created by a series of slip stitches, alternating the direction in which the hook is inserted into the stitch.

Instructions

1. Place your squares, side by side, with right sides facing up, making sure all the corresponding stitches align.

2. Place the hook into the edge stitch of one of the squares, inserting it from the outside in, and make a slip stitch (A, B).

3. Place the hook into the corresponding stitch on the other square, inserting the hook from the outside in, and make a slip stitch (C, D).

NOTE:

Be sure to keep the working yarn below (or under) your work.

ZIG-ZAG BORDER

Make a coordinating border by working
a slip stitch and chain 1 into every stitch
around the edge.

EMBELLISHING
THE EDGES

BORDERS AND TRIM MADE EASY:
SIMPLE HACKS FOR DECORATING THE EDGES

THE PERFECT BORDER

Adding a border is the perfect way to clean up and hide any ragged or wonky edges. It's also a great way to give your piece a polished look. Although not overly complicated, there are some tricky parts to adding borders, especially around the sides and corners. Hopefully these tips and techniques will help you tackle the borders with ease.

CORNER STITCHES

The second trickiest part of crocheting a border is knowing how many stitches to add into the corners. Quite often the recommended number is two—however, I find that adding three stitches into the corners creates the perfect sharp corner.

WORKING THE SIDE EDGE

Working a border is usually not an issue until you get to one of the sides with row ends. Not having defined stitches to work into can be tricky, but if you know how many stitches to add, it makes things much easier.

Here's how many border stitches to add when crocheting into the side of various basic stitches:

NUMBER OF BORDER STITCHES TO ADD

Stitch type	Number of stitches
Single crochet	1 st (A)
Half double crochet	2 sts (B)
Double crochet	3 sts (C)
Treble crochet	4 sts (D)

SIMPLE STITCH BORDER

Adding a simple slip stitch or single crochet border can give your piece a more polished look, and can help define the shape of your piece without adding extra detail. It also creates even working edges that come in handy when adding fringe or other finishing details.

REVERSE SINGLE CROCHET BORDER

We can't talk about simple borders and not mention one of the more unique stitches: the reverse single crochet aka the crab stitch.

Although it's made with nothing more than single crochet stitches, what makes this unique is that the stitches are worked in the opposite direction—instead of working right to left, they are worked left to right.

Instructions

1. Insert the hook into the stitch to the right and draw up a loop (A, B).

2. Yarn over and draw through all loops on the hook to finish the stitch (C).

TWISTED SINGLE CROCHET BORDER

If you like the look of a crab stitch but just can't seem to get the hang of working in reverse, then the twisted single crochet stitch might be for you. It creates virtually identical results to the crab stitch, but you're back to working in the standard direction.

Instructions

1. Insert the hook into the next stitch and draw up a loop.

2. Rotate the hook 360 degrees counterclockwise, twisting the loops (A, B).

3. Yarn over and draw through all loops on the hook to finish the stitch (C).

YARN FRINGE MADE EASY

I love the look of fringe on my crochet but adding it can be so time consuming. Cutting, attaching, trimming, cleaning up the aftermath... you get the idea! Fortunately there are some simple solutions you can implement—and if that still feels too much, I have included some no-cut fringe options that you can crochet with ease (see No-Cut Fringe).

PREPPING THE FRINGE

The most tedious part of adding fringe is having to cut each piece to the correct size. Here's what you can do to speed up this process.

Instructions

1. Get a strip of cardboard with a width approximately the length of the fringe required. Wrap the yarn around the cardboard as many times as pieces of fringe required. Be careful not to pull too tight as you don't want to stretch the yarn as you wrap (A).

2. Once you have made enough wraps (1 wrap = 1 piece of fringe) cut the end then cut through all the yarn wraps along one of the edges (B).

3. Use a crochet hook to attach the fringe to the work (C, D, E, F).

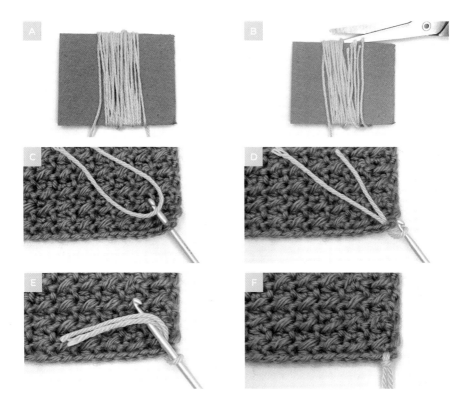

THE PERFECT CUT

Trimming the fringe to be perfectly straight can be extremely time consuming and tedious. Not to mention the mess that is left afterwards. Here's a tip that can not only help you get a perfectly straight fringe the first time, but also make clean-up a breeze.

For this you will need masking or painter's tape, at least 1in (2.5cm) wide, a rotary cutter or craft knife/blade, a metal ruler, and a cutting surface.

Instructions

1. Place the fringe on the cutting surface. Use a steamer or spray with water to get all the yarn pieces to lay flat (A).

2. Figure out where you would like your cut line to be and place the tape slightly below the cut line, holding the ends of the fringe down (B).

3. Place the ruler over the cut line and cut straight across using a rotary cutter or craft blade (C).

4. Peel off the tape with the trimmed ends for easy clean-up (D).

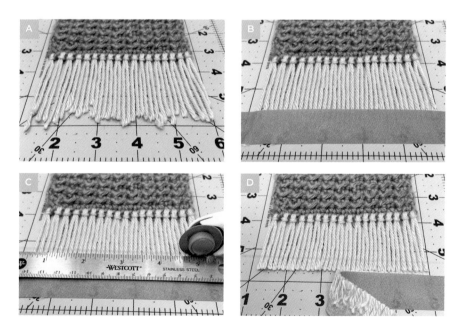

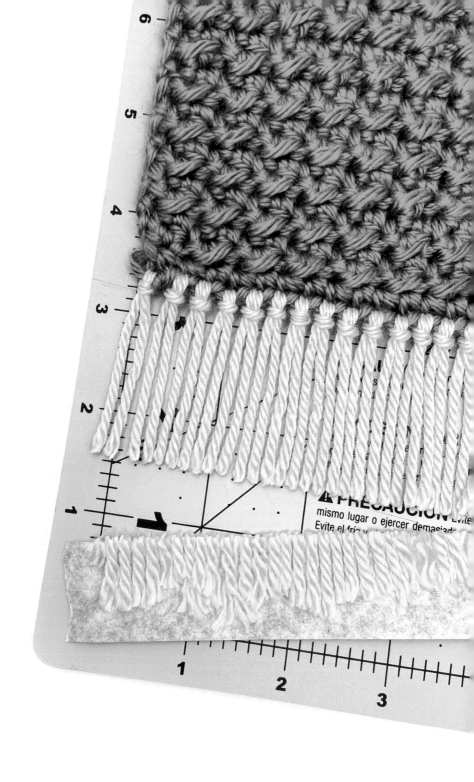

NO-CUT FRINGE

Love the idea of adding fringe but want to avoid all the cutting and attaching? Here are a couple great fringe options that can be crocheted directly to the edge of your project. Not only do these methods require no cutting or attaching, they are more durable than traditional cut fringe, making them a great option for projects that will get a lot of wear, such as garments and blankets.

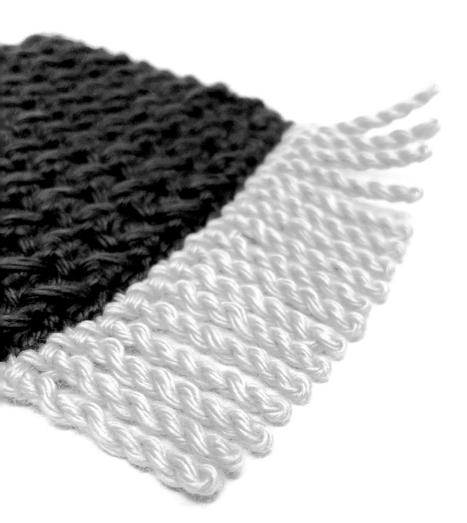

TWISTED FRINGE

The twisted fringe is a great alternative to a traditional string fringe. It is not only pretty, it's also more durable as it won't fray like regular string ends. The size of the fringe can easily be adjusted by pulling a longer loop or working a different number of twists.

Instructions

1. Slip stitch into the next stitch and pull up the working loop to be about twice the length of your desired fringe. Here it's 3in (7.5cm) (A).

2. Rotate the hook in the same direction, twisting the yarn until it becomes difficult to twist (15 to 20 times) (B).

3. Bring the twisted loop down, hold the middle with your thumb, then bring the loop back up and slip stitch back into the same stitch as in Step 1 (C).

4. Lift the thumb from the middle of the loop and watch it spring into the twist. Don't worry if your twist doesn't look perfect, gently tug or twirl the twist to even it out (D, E).

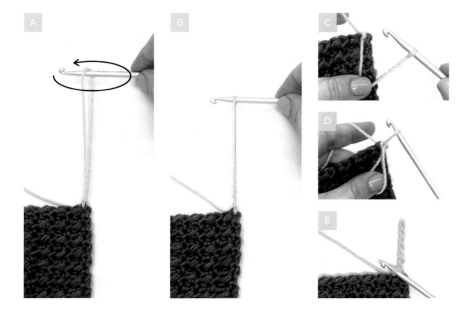

CROCHET FRINGE

Crochet fringe is a bold and versatile option to consider, especially when looking for fringe that makes a statement. Unlike traditional or twisted fringe, the strands here are fully crocheted, making this extremely durable. Crochet fringe can be worked directly onto the edge of your project or made separately and then seamed together.

Straight fringe

Instructions

1. Slip stitch into the next stitch and chain 8 (A). For a longer fringe, chain more stitches.

2. Slip stitch into second chain from the hook and into every remaining chain.

3. Slip stitch back into same stitch as in Step 1 (B).

4. Repeat Steps 1 to 3 until the end of the row.

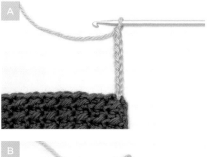

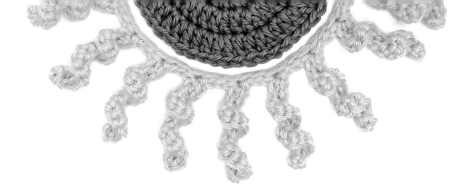

Corkscrew fringe

Instructions

1. Slip stitch into the next stitch and chain 10 (A).

2. Place two single crochet stitches into the second chain from the hook and into each remaining chain.

3. Slip stitch back into the same stitch as in Step 1 (B).

4. Repeat Steps 1 to 3 until the end of the row.

CUSTOMIZE THE CURL

———

Create a tighter coil by adding three or more stitches to each chain, or create a wider coil by replacing single crochet stitches with half double crochet or another tall stitch.

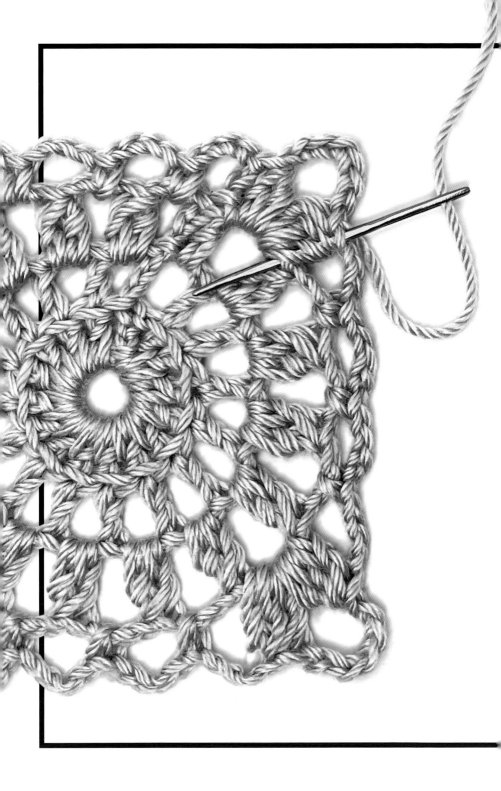

FLAWLESS
FINISH

FROM FASTENING OFF TO BLOCKING:
TIPS ON ACHIEVING THE PERFECT FINISH

FASTENING OFF

After making sure all your sides and edges are straight and smooth, and your rounds are seamless and perfect, don't drop the ball on finishing. Knowing how to fasten off is not just important for ensuring your piece remains looking great, but also for making sure your ends are secured and your work won't unravel.

INVISIBLE FINISH

If you struggle with making that last stitch or join look seamless, follow these simple steps.

Instructions

1. Do not slip stitch, break off the yarn and draw through the last stitch leaving a 5–6in (12.5–15cm) end.

2. Thread the end into a yarn needle. Skip a stitch, then insert the needle under both loops of the next stitch, front to back (A, B).

3. Insert the needle through the back loop of the last stitch, going front to back (C).

4. Gently pull on the end to tighten the new stitch (D).

WEAVING IN

It is important to weave in the yarn ends not only neatly but securely, so that they don't unravel while in use. Be sure to weave in different directions and don't weave too tightly.

Instructions

1. Weave the tail through the base of the stitches and along the posts, in various directions. The more you weave the more secure the ends will be (A, B).

2. For extra security add a tiny bit of fabric glue to each end to really keep everything in place.

> **IMPORTANT**
>
> *When weaving the ends keep similar tension to the overall piece. Don't weave too tightly as it can create puckering in your finished piece.*

LACY STITCHES

Weave your ends through the middle of the stitches, moving along the length of the stitch. This will assure the tails remain hidden and won't interfere with the look of the finished piece.

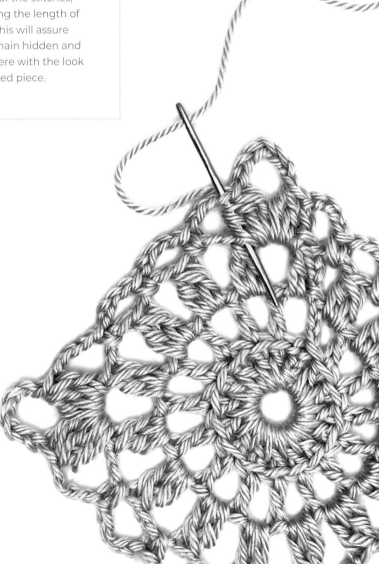

BLOCKING SIMPLIFIED

Blocking is a method of using moisture to gently stretch and mold your finished piece into the correct shape and size. Although many typically skip this step, I can't stress its importance in making your final pieces look as perfect as possible.

STEAM BLOCKING

The concept of traditional wet blocking always seemed intimidating, not to mention time consuming, as you have to soak the entire piece and then wait for it to dry. Steam blocking is a simple and time-saving alternative that works great for natural fibers such as cotton, wool, and linen, but can also be used with acrylic. Just be sure not to let the steamer touch the yarn.

Instructions

1. Pin down the piece, stretching it into the correct shape and size (A).

2. Hover the steamer approximately 1–2in (2.5–5cm) over the piece, continuously moving back and forth (B).

3. While steaming you may continue to move and stretch the piece to even out any wonky stitches, or smooth out any imperfections.

4. Once everything is in place and the piece is damp, allow to cool and dry completely before removing the pins.

> **! IMPORTANT**
>
> *Do not allow the steamer to touch the yarn.*

before blocking

after blocking

CROCHET
CHEAT SHEET

CHARTS, TABLES AND HELPFUL YARN AND
HOOK INFORMATION ALL IN ONE PLACE

ABBREVIATIONS (US TERMS)

blo - back loop only

ch - chain stitch

dc - double crochet

dec - decrease

dtr - double treble crochet

fdc - foundation double crochet

fhdc - foundation half double crochet

flo - front loop only

fs - foundation stitch

fsc - foundation single crochet

ftr - foundation treble crochet

hdc - half double crochet

inc - increase

mr - magic ring

rep - repeat

sc - single crochet

sk - skip

slst - slip stitch

sp - space

st - stitch

stsc - stacked single crochet

tog - together

tr - treble crochet

yo - yarn over

[ ] - repeat sequence in brackets the number of times stated

US TO UK CONVERSION

This book is written using US terminology. Although UK may use similar wording, some terms refer to completely different stitches, which can be confusing. Here's a list of stitches to keep in mind.

US	UK
single crochet (sc)	double crochet (dc)
half double crochet (hdc)	half treble crochet (htr)
double crochet (dc)	treble crochet (tr)
treble crochet (tr)	double treble crochet (dtr)
double treble crochet (dtr)	triple treble crochet (ttr)

CHOOSING THE BEST HOOK

US	UK	MM
Lace	1-2 ply	2-2.25
Fingering	2 ply	2.5-3
Sock	3 ply	3-3.5
Sport weight	4 ply	3.5-4.5
Light worsted	DK/8 ply	4-5
Worsted	Aran/10 ply	4.5-6.5
Bulky	Chunky/Rug	6-9
Super bulky	Super chunky	9-15
Jumbo	Ultra roving	15+

HOOK SIZES

MM	US
2	–
2.25	B-1
2.5	–
2.75	C-2
3	–
3.25	D-3
3.5	E-4
3.75	F-5
4	G-6
4.25	G
4.5	7
5	H-8
5.5	I-9
6	J-10
6.5	K-10.5
7	–
8	L-11
9	M/N-13
10	N/P-15
12.75	–
15	P/Q
16	Q
19	S
25	T/U/X

STEEL (MICRO) HOOK SIZES

MM	US
3.5	00
3.25	0
2.75	1
2.7	00
2.55	0
2.35	1
2.25/2.20	2
2.1	3
2	4
1.9	5
1.8	6
1.7	5
1.65	7
1.6	6
1.5	8/7/2
1.4	9/8
1.3	10
1.25	9/4
1.1	11
1	12/6
0.95	13
0.9	18/8
0.85	13
0.75	14/10
0.6	12

HOW MUCH YARN DO YOU NEED?

Yarn weight	#1	#2	#3	#4	#5	#6	#7
	250–325yd 229–297m	225–300yd 206–274m	200–250yd 183–229m	200–225yd 183–206m	150–200yd 137–183m	125–150yd 114–137m	30–70yd 27–64m
	525–825yd 480–754m	450–625yd 411–572m	400–500yd 366–457m	375–500yd 343–457m	275–375yd 251–343m	250–375yd 229–343m	125–225yd 114–206m
	350–850yd 320–777m	300–450yd 274–411m	275–400yd 251–366m	230–375yd 210–343m	250–350yd 229–320m	225–275yd 206–251m	175–200yd 160–183m
	550–850yd 503–777m	450–700yd 411–640m	400–650yd 366–594m	375–600yd 343–549m	350–500yd 320–457m	350–475yd 320–434m	300–400yd 274–366m
	3000–3500yd 2743–3200m	1700–2650yd 1554–2423m	1100–1650yd 1006–1509m	1100–1650yd 1006–1509m	950–1200yd 869–1097m	825–1175yd 754–1074m	800–1150yd 732–1052m

ABOUT THE AUTHOR

Anna Leyzina is a graphic designer, crocheter and the one-woman-show behind The Knotty Boss. Born in Kyiv, Ukraine, she emigrated to the United States, with her family, when she was a teen. Anna attended the University of the Arts (Philadelphia) graduating with a BFA in graphic design and then worked as a professional designer for over 15 years.

Spending most of her days in an office she wanted a plant to liven up her desk. Unfortunately, as a self-proclaimed plant-killer, she knew her only chance at plant happiness meant the plant had to be fake. She turned to the Internet to look for fake plant ideas and discovered a world of amigurumi cacti. Although never having crocheted before she was adamant about trying to make one of those cacti. The very next day she ran to the store, got her first hook and green yarn, then spent weeks on YouTube trying to figure out what in the world a magic ring was.

Fast forward to today and Anna's love for crochet has only gotten stronger. She's found passion in designing crochet patterns, creating a series of popular marketing tools for crafters, and sharing her viral crochet tips and tutorials.

She currently resides in the Philadelphia area with her yarn and over 100 real plants... she can actually keep those alive now!

You can find Anna and her work on social media @TheKnottyBoss or www.theknottyboss.com

my first crochet cactus

ACKNOWLEDGMENTS

A huge thank you to my friends and family for all your love and for keeping me sane during these crazy months.

Thanks to the wonderful team at David and Charles for this amazing opportunity and making this book a reality. I appreciate all of your hard work, guidance, and most of all patience... lots of patience!

A big thank you to Yarnspirations for your generosity and yarn support.

The biggest thank you to the wonderful crochet community and everyone who has supported me and my work throughout the years. I appreciate you all more than I can express.

Dedicated to my parents, Ekaterina and David, who left everything they knew behind to give me a better chance... and then didn't freak out when I decided to go to art school.

In loving memory of my friend, and one of the first TKB supporters, Richard Knott.

INDEX

ISBN-13: 9781446313206 paperback
ISBN-13: 9781446313213 EPUB
ISBN-13: 9781446313220 PDF

This book has been printed on paper from approved suppliers and made from pulp from sustainable sources.

MIX
Paper | Supporting responsible forestry
FSC
www.fsc.org
FSC® C118234

Printed in Bosnia and Herzegovina by GPS Group for David and Charles, Ltd, Suite A, Tourism House, Pynes Hill, Exeter, EX2 5WS

10 9 8 7 6 5 4

Publishing Director: Ame Verso
Senior Commissioning Editor: Sarah Callard
Managing Editor: Jeni Chown
Technical Editor: Sam Winkler
Copy Editor: Marie Clayton
Head of Design: Anna Wade
Designer: Anna Leyzina, Sam Staddon and Jo Webb
Pre-press Designer: Susan Reansbury
Photography: Anna Leyzina
Production Manager: Beverley Richardson

David and Charles publishes high-quality books on a wide range of subjects. For more information visit www.davidandcharles.com.

Share your makes with us on social media using #dandcbooks and follow us on Facebook and Instagram by searching for @dandcbooks.

Layout of the digital edition of this book may vary depending on reader hardware and display settings.